ON THE CASE!

CYBERSECURITY EXPERTS

Madison Capitano

ROURKE'S SCHOOL to HOME CONNECTIONS
BEFORE AND DURING READING ACTIVITIES

Before Reading: *Building Background Knowledge and Vocabulary*

Building background knowledge can help children process new information and build upon what they already know. Before reading a book, it is important to tap into what children already know about the topic. This will help them develop their vocabulary and increase their reading comprehension.

Questions and Activities to Build Background Knowledge:
1. Look at the front cover of the book and read the title. What do you think this book will be about?
2. What do you already know about this topic?
3. Take a book walk and skim the pages. Look at the table of contents, photographs, captions, and bold words. Did these text features give you any information or predictions about what you will read in this book?

Vocabulary: *Vocabulary Is Key to Reading Comprehension*
Use the following directions to prompt a conversation about each word.
- Read the vocabulary words.
- What comes to mind when you see each word?
- What do you think each word means?

Vocabulary Words:
- artifacts
- hacker
- encrypted
- malware
- firewall
- virus

During Reading: *Reading for Meaning and Understanding*

To achieve deep comprehension of a book, children are encouraged to use close reading strategies. During reading, it is important to have children stop and make connections. These connections result in deeper analysis and understanding of a book.

Close Reading a Text
During reading, have children stop and talk about the following:
- Any confusing parts
- Any unknown words
- Text to text, text to self, text to world connections
- The main idea in each chapter or heading

Encourage children to use context clues to determine the meaning of any unknown words. These strategies will help children learn to analyze the text more thoroughly as they read.

When you are finished reading this book, turn to the next-to-last page for **After Reading Questions** and an **Activity**.

TABLE OF CONTENTS

On the Case 4

Identity Theft 8

Hidden Malware 14

Cyber-Detectives 21

Memory Game 30

Index 31

After Reading Questions 31

Activity 31

About the Author 32

ON THE CASE

Think about the information that is important for daily life: passwords, account numbers, photos, addresses, and more. It is all stored on computers. Cybersecurity experts protect data and keep it out of the hands of criminals!

CYBER-WHAT?

The prefix *cyber-* means "having to do with computers and other digital devices." Some words with *cyber-* are *cyberspace, cybercriminal, cyberattack, cybercafe,* and *cybersecurity*!

4

Cybersecurity experts know all about computers. They use advanced searching and coding skills to keep information safe, to stop computer bugs, and to help solve crimes.

LEARN THE LINGO

Coding works by using different computer languages to give commands. HTML, Java, Perl, and Python are examples of different computer languages that programmers use to create everything from websites to games to apps.

IDENTITY THEFT

A company gets an alert. A **hacker** is trying to steal customers' identities! Hackers look for credit card numbers and other information that identifies people. Cybersecurity experts are on the case.

» **hacker** (HAK-ur): someone with special skills for getting into a computer system

Over ten million people have their identities stolen every year by hackers. Banks, social media companies, and stores are all at risk.

Companies hire cybersecurity experts to find weaknesses in their computer systems. Experts hack into systems to find ways to make them safer. This is called ethical hacking.

TIP YOUR HAT

Not all hackers steal identities. There are *white hat* hackers and *black hat* hackers. Black hat hackers use their skills to commit cybercrimes. White hat hackers find flaws in computer systems and work to fix them.

Luckily, cybersecurity experts at the company were able to improve the system before the hacker could steal any information. They set up a **firewall** that stopped the crime from happening.

» **firewall** (FIRE-wawl): software or hardware that creates a barrier between a computer network and external sources, such as hackers

12

HIDDEN MALWARE

When an employee sees an email that looks like it's from their boss, they have no idea it's actually **malware**! Cybersecurity experts are on the case.

» **malware** (MAL-wair): software that is meant to harm or create problems

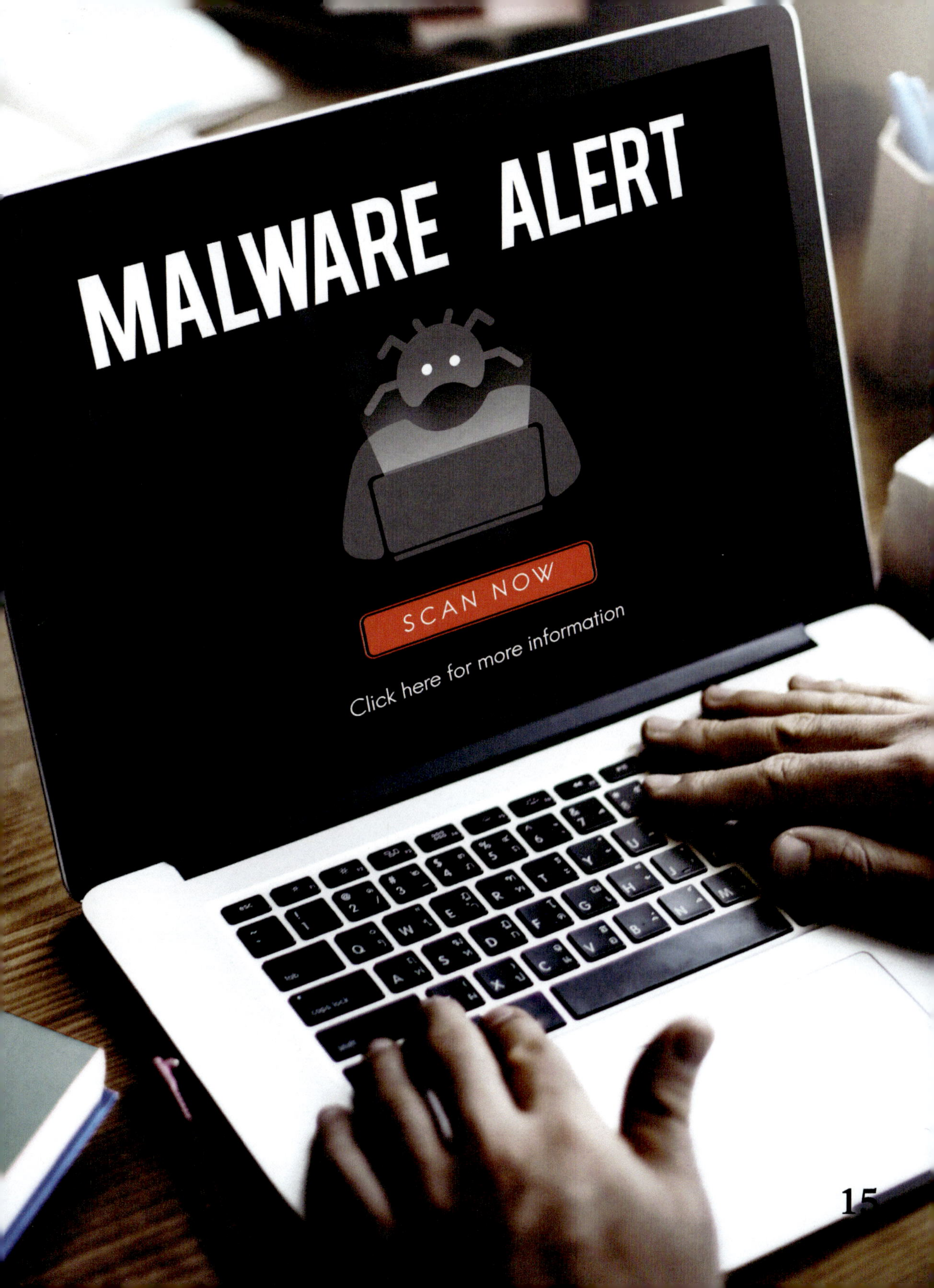
MALWARE ALERT
SCAN NOW
Click here for more information

When a hacker sends a fake message carrying dangerous software, it is called phishing (FISH-ing). Phishing is one way hackers can get a **virus** into a computer network. When the user clicks on the hacker's message, the damage is done.

A CREEPER

The first computer attack came as a virus in 1971. Users were surprised when their screens started to show "I'm the creeper: catch me if you can."

» **virus** (VYE-ruhs): a hidden computer program that is designed to harm a computer system or steal data

17

Some cybersecurity experts are malware analysts. It is their job to find out what malware is doing and stop it.

The fake email contained a virus that would have erased **encrypted** information. Malware analysts warned everyone in the company not to open the email. They found the virus and deleted it before it could cause harm.

» **encrypted** (en-KRIP-ted): converted into a code to protect from unauthorized access

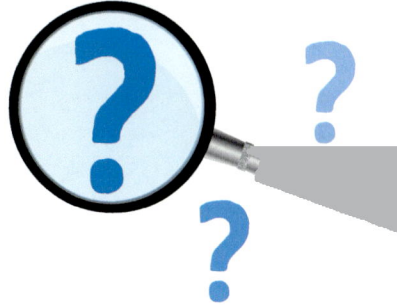

CYBER-DETECTIVES

After disappearing for 30 years, a killer is back. The criminal is sending mysterious messages to the police.

Cybersecurity experts, called cyber-forensic investigators, are on the case.

Cyber-forensic investigators are high-tech detectives. They use computers to find evidence to help catch criminals.

They look for, and examine, digital **artifacts**.

» **artifacts** (AHR-tuh-fakts): information that gets left behind when a person uses a computer or another device

Emails, texts, and files travel between devices as invisible packages.

These packages contain more than just photos or emojis. They also contain leftover information about where the data came from, who has used it, and how it was made. This information is often called a digital fingerprint.

The killer's biggest mistake was using technology to send messages to police. A cyber-forensic investigator immediately found digital artifacts in them. Digital fingerprints allowed police to easily find the criminal's name and location.

With more than 17 billion devices connected to the internet, cybersecurity experts have a big job keeping everyone's information safe.

They work hard to stay a step ahead of hackers and cybercriminals. Cybersecurity experts are on the case!

MEMORY GAME

Look at the pictures. What do you remember reading on the pages where each image appeared?

INDEX

coding 7
computer(s) 4, 7, 8, 11, 12, 17, 22
criminal(s) 4, 21, 22, 26
data 4, 17, 25
identities 8, 11
network 12, 17
police 21, 26
social media 11

AFTER READING QUESTIONS

1. What is it called when people give computers commands?
2. What are two different computer languages?
3. What is a white hat hacker?
4. What is one way cybersecurity experts can stop hackers?
5. What is it called when a hacker sends a fake email for someone to open?

ACTIVITY

Create your own secret code to protect private messages between you and a friend. Name your code and write down or memorize the encryption key. Then, use your code to send messages to each other.

ABOUT THE AUTHOR

Madison Capitano is a writer in Columbus, Ohio, who loves to watch mystery shows! She knows a little about computers, but she leaves big jobs to the pros! Madison used to read books to her little brother and sister all the time. Now she loves to write books for other kids to enjoy.

© 2021 Rourke Educational Media

All rights reserved. No part of this book may be reproduced or utilized in any form or by any means, electronic or mechanical including photocopying, recording, or by any information storage and retrieval system without permission in writing from the publisher.

www.rourkeeducationalmedia.com

PHOTO CREDITS: page 1: ©peshkov / iStock; page 5: ©TommL / iStock; page 6: ©DragonImages / iStock; page 9: ©solarseven / iStock; page 10: ©napocska / Shutterstock; page 13: ©MF3d / iStock; page 15: ©Rawpixel.com / Shutterstock; page 16: ©solitude72 / iStock; page 19: ©Vertigo3d / iStock; page 20: ©DAVID PULLIAM / Newscom; page 23: ©gorodenkoff / iStock; page 24: ©ALLVISIONN / iStock; page 27: ©JEFF TUTTLE / Newscom; page 28: ©sanjeri / iStock; caution tape: ©tcenitelkrasoti / Pixabay; magnifying glass: ©Pixaline / Pixabay

Edited by: Kim Thompson
Cover design by: Kathy Walsh
Interior design by: Sara Radka

Library of Congress PCN Data

Cybersecurity Experts / Madison Capitano
(On the Case!)
ISBN 978-1-73163-813-7 (hard cover)
ISBN 978-1-73163-890-8 (soft cover)
ISBN 978-1-73163-967-7 (e-Book)
ISBN 978-1-73164-044-4 (e-Pub)
Library of Congress Control Number: 2020930181

Rourke Educational Media
Printed in the United States of America
02-3082211937

32